A CIP catalogue record for this title is available from the British Library.

ISBN   (1527222497)

First Published (2018)

www.josephhopkins.co.uk

This book belongs to

....

BUSY BODIES

for creative champions

Activity 1

What mini sports people will you make?

Activity 2

Make your final sports busy body,
name them and tell us what they enjoy.

_____

_____

_____

_____

_____

Activity 3

What water sports are going on today?

Activity 4

Can you get Pucky through the maze and to his puck?

– Finish me!

Maths - 2B- Uses pencil accurately to move in straight lines and turns.

Activity 5

HUFF

Huff needs a new coloured kit, can you help?

Hall
of
frame.

Can you
Fill in the
empty
frames?

Activity 7

The crowd is very quiet, can you add them in and get them cheering?

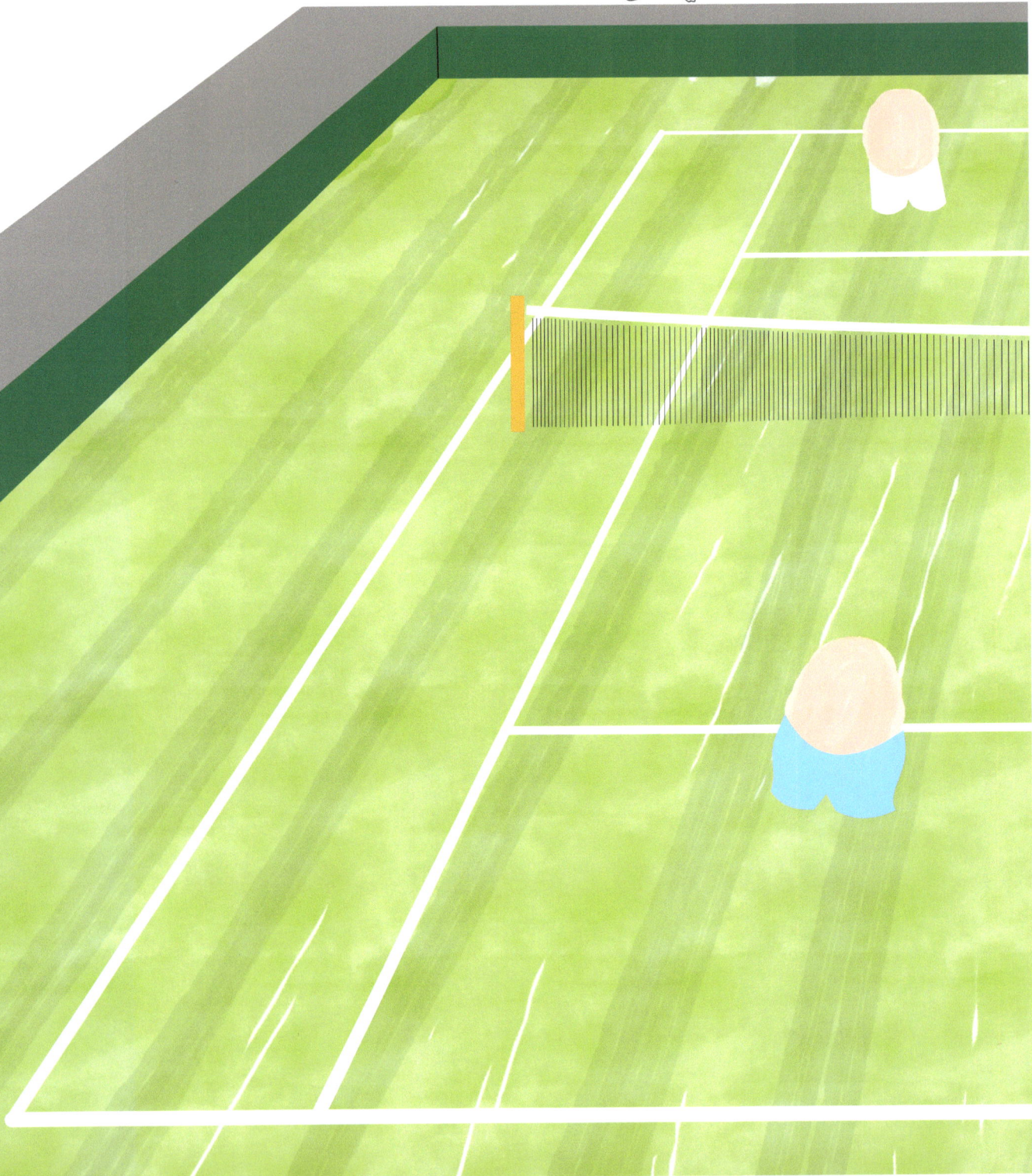

What happened in the match?

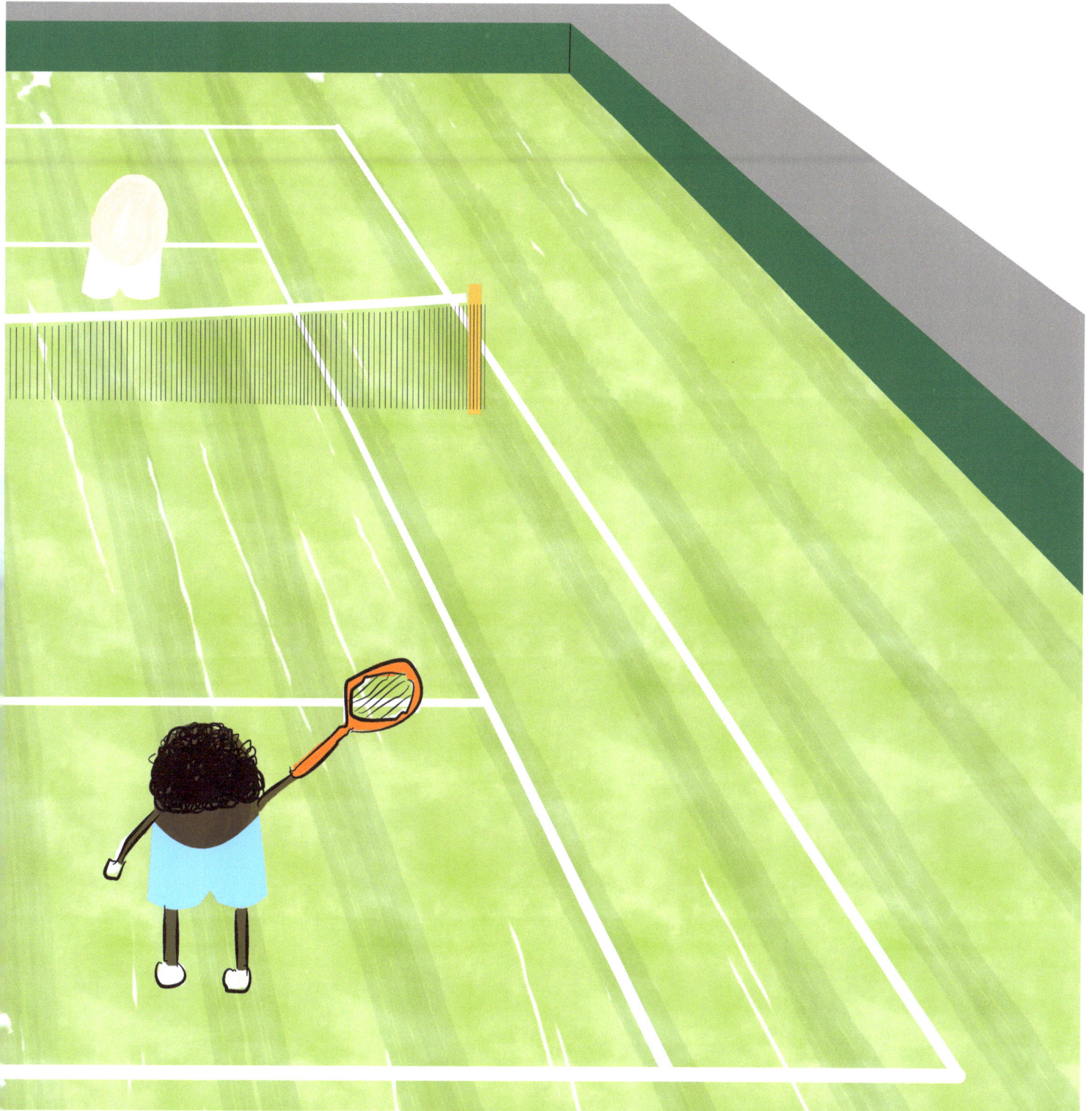

Activity 8

These kits need finishing. Can you colour them, add your surname and put on numbers between 1 – 10?

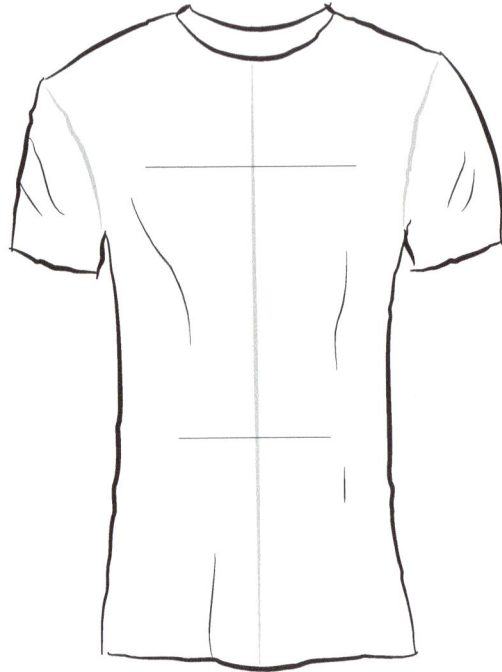

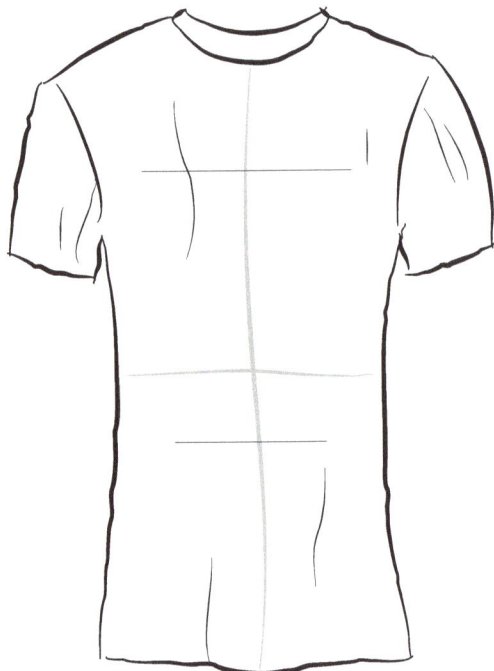

Phillips

8

English - 1C - Writes all the letter shapes of their name.
Maths - 1C - Writes numbers to 10 consistently.

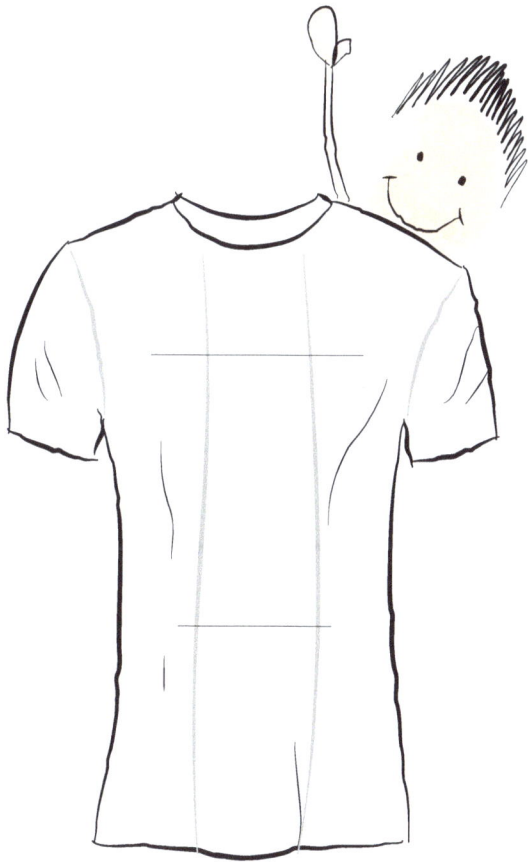

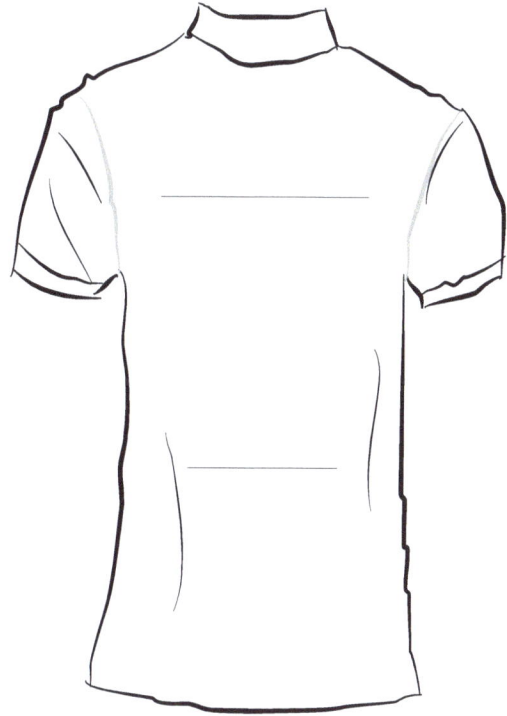

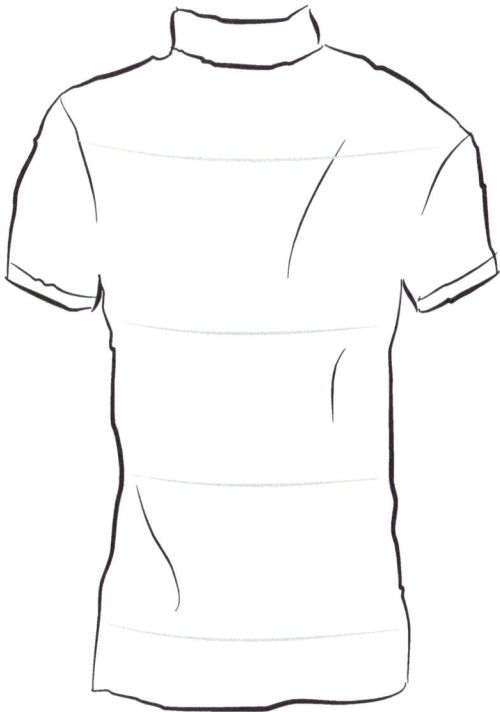

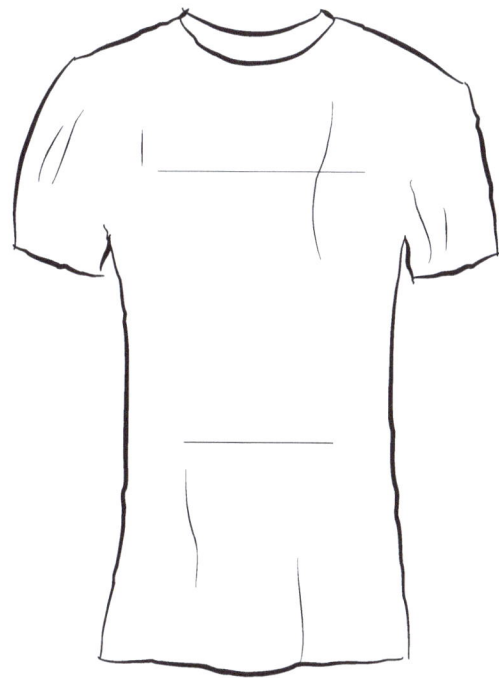

Activity 9

The Busy Bodies love poetry. Can you complete this
Acrostic poem below linking it to sport?

B _____

U _____

S _____

Y _____

B _____

O _____

D _____

I _____

E _____

S _____

English - 1A - Writes in simple structures including poetry.

Can you create your own Acrostic Poem below?

_____

_____

_____

_____

_____

_____

_____

_____

_____

Activity 10

Can you solve these scoreboard sums?

20:03

11 + 7 =

12 + 6 =

14 + 5 =

15 + 7 =

17 + 8 =

Score master

Maths - 2B - Using concrete aids - add two digit number to single digit.

Can you solve these scoreboard sums?

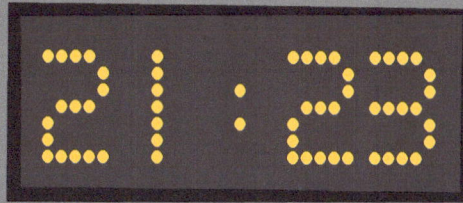

21:23

14 + 9 =

24 + 8 =

22 + 7 =

27 + 6 =

28 + 7 =

Score master

Activity 11

The Busy Bodies are training. Can you find the shapes and colour them in two colours?

Like this !

Don't forget to finish the Busy Bodies too!

Activity 12

This is Ron the rugby rhino. Could you colour him in and then on the next page write a short story about playing rugby?

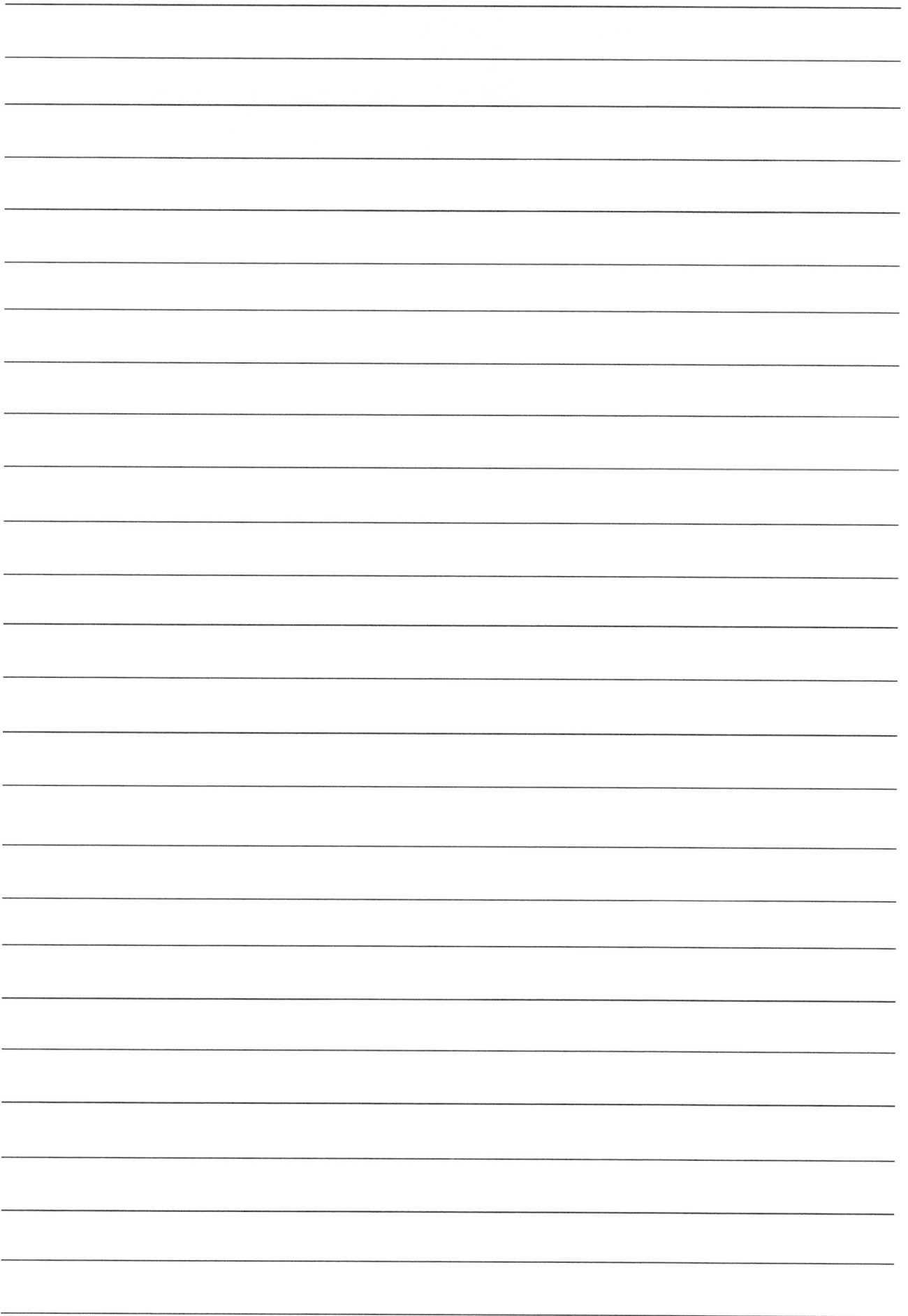

Activity 13   The Busy Bodies have plans to build a big stadium. Can you colour in the design and finish the characters?

Can you show the Busy Bodies running a race?

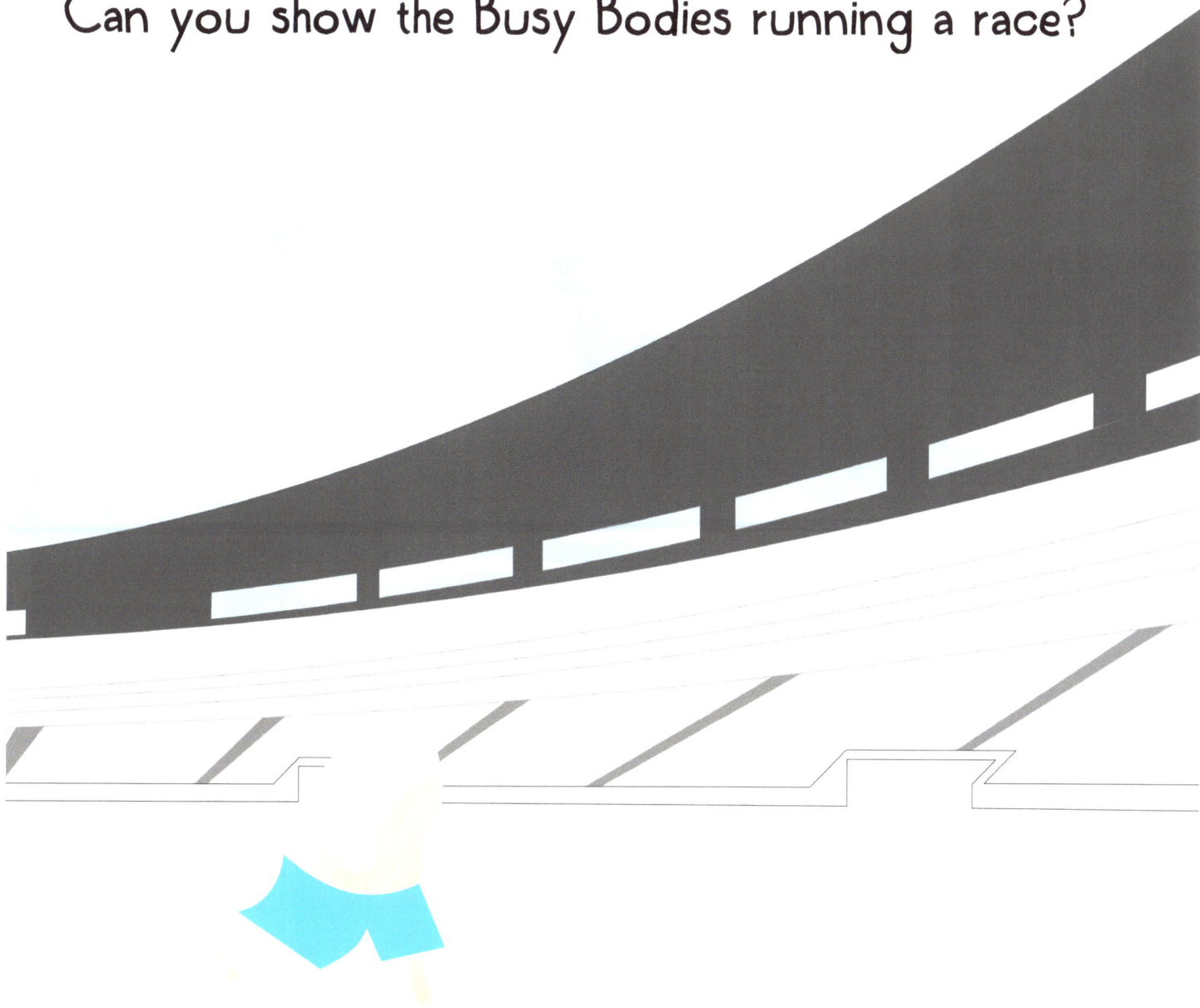

WORLD FACTS

ALASKA

NORTH AMERICA

North America
The Golden Gate Bridge is a suspension bridge connecting San Francisco Bay and the Pacific Ocean.

Canada
The National Hockey League (NHL) was founded on November 22, 1917.

USA
The NBA is made up of two conferences, East and West conferences in the USA

U.K

England
Wembley stadium has 90,000 seats and NO obstructed views.

Can you find out any other interesting sports facts from around the world?

South America
The nine nations that have the Amazon rainforest in their borders are:
Brazil, Peru, Columbia, Venezuela, Ecuador, Bolivia, Guyana, Suriname and French Guiana.

Mexico
Mexico has produced more world boxing champions than any other nation.

SOUTH AMERICA

Brazil
PSG paid Barcelona a world record 222 million to sign Neymar Jr.

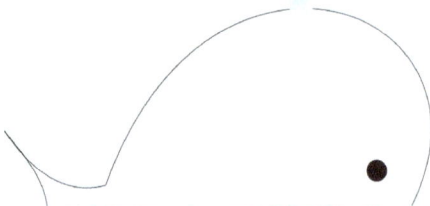

Can you find where five famous sports personalities come from in the world?

RUSSIA

Russia
Russia was awarded to be hosts of the FIFA World Cup in 2018. It is the first time they were named hosts of this event.

Switzerland
Roger Federer has won the most tennis singles grand slams in history for a male player.

JAPAN

China
China starts training its gymnasts from the age of four.

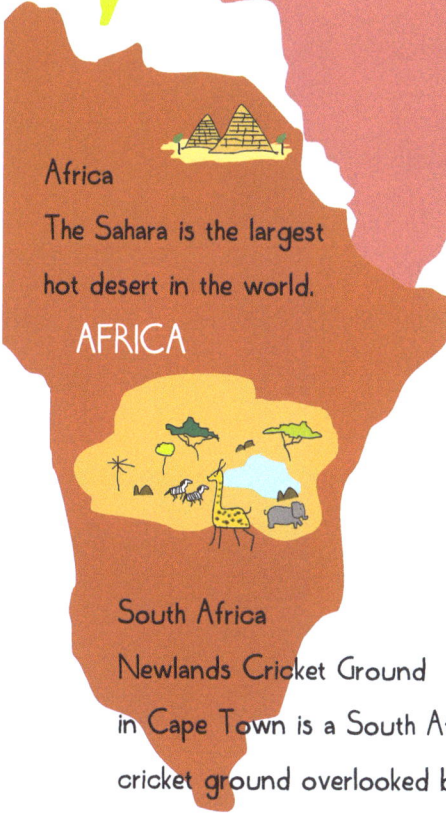

Africa
The Sahara is the largest hot desert in the world.

AFRICA

India
The Indian Premier League (IPL), is a professional Twenty20 cricket league.

South Africa
Newlands Cricket Ground in Cape Town is a South African cricket ground overlooked by table mountain.

AUSTRALIA

The four major tennis tournaments take place in Melbourne, London, Paris and New York.

New Zealand
New Zealand became the first Rugby international team in the professional era to go all season unbeaten.

Activity 14

These Busy Bodies may be good at their sport but they need your help to complete these tricky questions.

Can you use the red words to complete these sentences?

or   because   if   when   so

1. Tomorrow, we can't go to the park _____ it is going to rain.

2. We had better get home _____ we will get in trouble with Mum and Dad.

3. _____ you get changed quickly, you can play in goal today.

4. I can't decide what team to support _____ you decide for me.

5. I wonder _____ we will find out who is the fastest runner?

Can you tick which tense is correct for the sentence?

Sentence	Past tense	Future tense
Busy Body Ben ate a banana for energy.		
The Busy Bodies are off to a big match tomorrow.		
Busy Body Bella went out to play golf.		

Activity 15

Can you create a Busy Body that is like you and write some descriptive sentences describing the characters appearance and personality?

_____

_____

_____

_____

_____

_____

_____

_____

_____

_____

Activity 16

Can you research and label the main muscles on the body below?

THE MUSCLES IN MY BODY

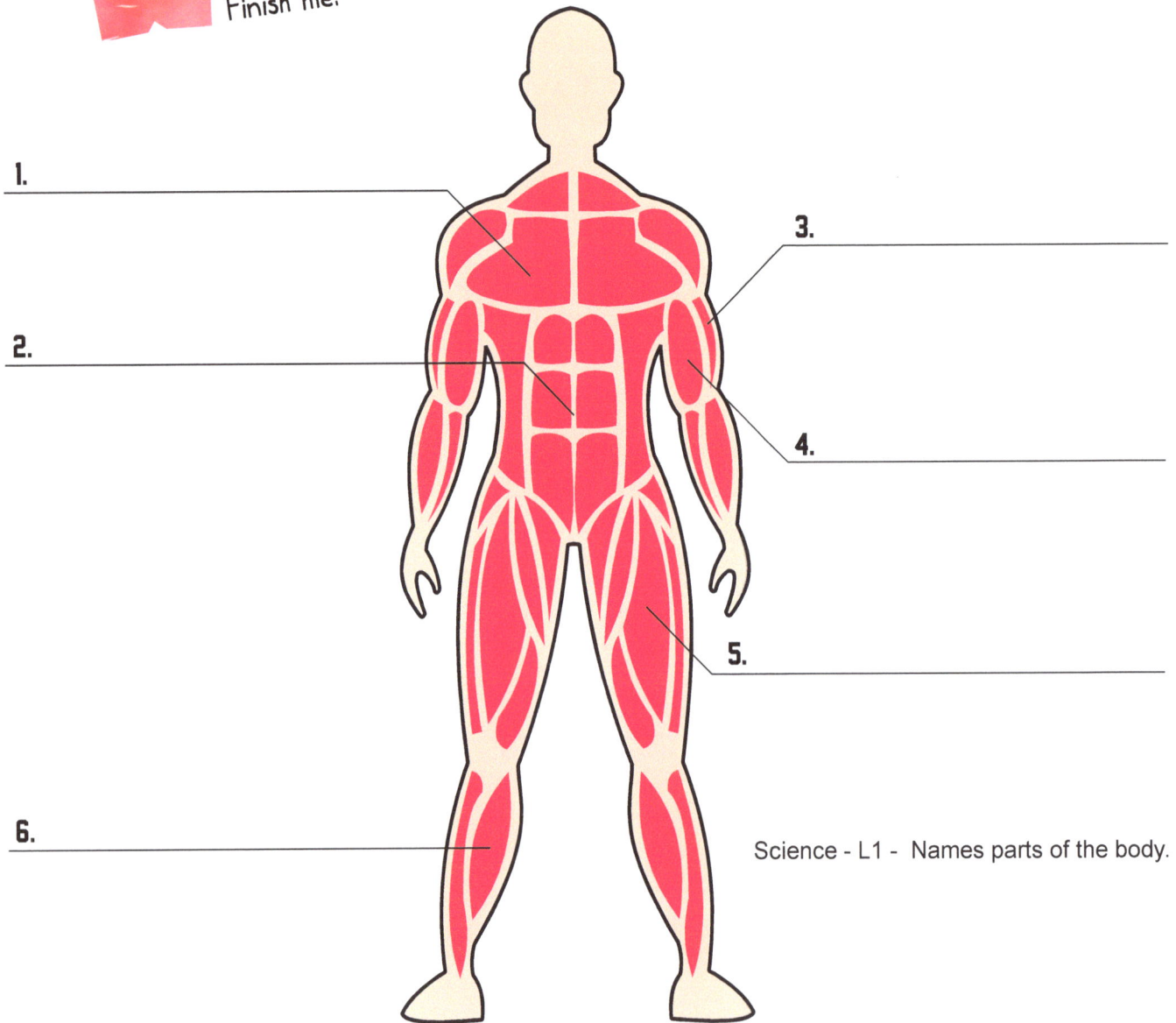

Finish me!

1.

2.

3.

4.

5.

6.

Science - L1 - Names parts of the body.

WORD BANK

quadriceps   pectorals   biceps   triceps

rectus abdominis   gastrocnemius

Activity 17

Can you spot the 9 differences between the two images and circle them?

The big game.

Busy Body Ben was super excited. It was his first game for his new school football team. Sure Ben felt a little bit nervous but he was looking forward to playing his favourite sport.

As Ben arrived in the changing room he could see all the fresh kits hanging along the wall. He was going to be wearing his lucky number 9. Soon the other Busy Bodies players began to arrive. Bill, Brad and Bobby had been really good to Ben since he started at the new school so he felt happy sitting amongst them to get ready for the big game.

Mr Bradshaw came in once the boys were ready.

"Right lads. Big game for us tonight. Lots of the people have stayed behind to watch and they are hoping to see us win."

Ben started to feel a little bit worried knowing a lot of people would be watching. As Mr Bradshaw continued talking, Ben whispered to Bobby who was sat beside him on the bench. "Bobby, are you nervous?"

"No, it's going to be great Ben and so are you. Let your feet do the talking." Bobby quietly replied.

Mr Bradshaw finished his tactics using the large white board and Ben was starting upfront as striker.

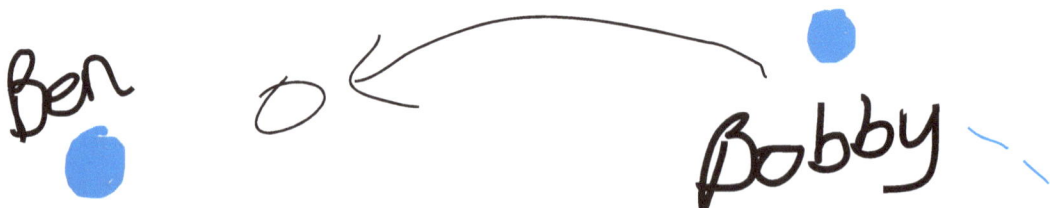

Ben

Bobby

The first half was a pretty boring half of football as games go. Neither team had played to their potential and the crowd were starting to get a bit restless watching. Busy Body Ben had made some really neat touches but had not yet had a shot at the other teams goal.

Brad got a yellow card for a naughty tackle and Bill had been great playing as a defender.

Half time arrived with the score at 0-0. Mr Bradshaw was pretty calm in his half time team talk. He told the boys to relax and to play with more enjoyment, freedom and said if you get a chance, hit it!

As the second half got underway Ben noticed that is Mum and Dad had arrived and were watching from behind the goal. Ben now felt even more determined to work hard and score.

The second half was a much better game. The other team hit the woodwork twice and Brad had a brilliant header cleared off the goal line. The referee signalled that there would be three minutes of injury time and the game looked like it would be a finishing as a draw.

Just then Ben made a run off of the back of the last defender and was spotted by his good friend Bobby who had the ball. Bobby's pass was perfect. He clipped it high over the defence and into the path of Ben who was galloping towards goal.

It then felt like time stopped. Ben had lots of thoughts run through his head about what to do now he was one on one with the big keeper. Just then he remembered Mr Bradshaw's final words at half time. HIT IT! So he did. He struck the ball as hard and as sweet as he had ever struck a ball. It flew into the goal like an absolute rocket! The whistle went and Ben had got the winner! The nickname 'Big Ben' seemed perfect for the striker who scored in the big game.

Activity 18

Can you answer these questions below about the Busy Bodies story on the last two pages?

1. What shirt number did Ben wear and why was it a good number?

_____

_____

_____

2. How did Ben feel when he knew a lot of people would be watching?

_____

_____

_____

3. What did Mr Bradshaw tell the team to do at half time?

_____

_____

THE
END